Ultimate Guide to Becoming Your Best on Dialysis

BANJI AWOSIKA

PREFACE

My father and every one of his siblings had hypertension. At the time I was deciding my career path, he had lost a SIBLING due to complications of hypertension. I had always known I wanted to help people as who had same health issues like my dad. Due to my academic quests, he saw the potential for me to become a doctor. After a few years in medical school, I left for a year to improve my financial situation. Amongst my jobs was working as a cab driver in London, UK. I actually fell in love with medicine after I left it for a while. So I finally came to the realization that this was what I actually was called to do.

Taking care and servicing the needs that people have, educating people and showing them how to get healthier, lessening and eventually eliminating the need for medication. Taking care and servicing the needs that people have, as well as hearing from the families of the patients that I am taking care of were amongst the most rewarding aspects that I experienced as a physician. Seeing the impact on their lives was also very rewarding. When the mother of a patient comes back and tells me they lost ten pounds and that they are off medications themselves; that blesses the socks off of me. The whole idea is to create ambassadors of this message, from the patients to the staffs that work with me as well as the families of the patients. That's when I can really make a difference.

This book is meant for patients receiving dialysis or patients with advanced kidney disease not yet on dialysis or family members of patients receiving dialysis that want to solve the challenge of insufficient and inefficient communication from dialysis care providers including their nephrologists as well as avoiding frequent hospitalizations as well as the dialysis drain. Let's get started.

++++++++++++++++++++++++++++++++++++++

Banji Awosika 08-Oct-2016

TABLE OF CONTENTS

CHAPTER ONE

The kidneys and disease

What is the Importance of Kidneys?

Kidneys are important part of waste removal from the body. As the body has used parts of the nutrients that we consume that it finds usable for various processes in the body, the remainder of that nutrient has to be eliminated from the body and this is done via the lungs, the gut, kidneys, the skin. Kidneys are also very important for adding things to the system that is they have a synthetic function. These include erythropoietin which is a red blood cells stimulating agent necessary for carrying oxygen to the cells required to burn glucose and other fuels in order to produce energy and heat for the body. Another product of the synthetic function of kidneys is active-form vitamin D. Many of the chemicals in the body have to stay within a specific range and this is referred to as homeostasis. The kidney is very instrumental in maintaining various chemicals in the body within this range. Otherwise, if it is too high it will be toxic chemical to the body and if it is too low it will be an ineffective chemical in the body. The blood pressure is also very important and this reflects the pressure within the blood chamber in the body and the regulation of this pressure is a very important function of the kidney.

Effects of Disease On Kidneys

25% of the blood volume circulates through the kidneys every minute and because of this, it acts as a very large filter and of course as a filter, it is very susceptible to the content of the blood it is filtering. Disease state anywhere in the body affects the kidneys, directly or indirectly. Indirectly, various chemicals stimulated by the disease affect kidney function. Disease state itself directly also may release chemicals that affect the kidney function. The effects on kidneys can be an acute situation or the beginning of a chronic kidney problem. Effects on the kidneys also affects the outcome and the prognosis of the disease state itself.

The Effects of Kidneys on Disease

Less than optimal kidney function worsens the prognosis of almost all diseases. Kidney function is also very important in deciding what dose of medications should be used to treat the said disease and the type of medication to be used is also strongly determined by the kidney function. These factors all contribute to the optimal and effective management of many diseases.

Habits That Lead To Kidney Disease?

Various diseases are common causes of kidney disease. More specifically diabetes and hypertension. These diseases are significantly affected by lifestyle and our lifestyle comprise of habits that we have, as well as habits that we unfortunately do not have. Habits that we have that lead to diabetes, hypertension and ultimately kidney disease includes:

- Excessive intake of fatty foods especially saturated fats and cholesterol
- Excessive amounts of starch based calorie consumption, much more than we expend in our daily exercise and physical activity, in terms of calories that are used up during physical activity and exercise.
- Insufficient amount of vegetables and fruits with the consequent insufficient amount of phytochemicals i.e. plants chemicals that are very important in anti-inflammation in our system.
- Sedentary lifestyle with very low amounts of physical activity which is very necessary for bone health, muscle health, and overall well-being.
- Cigarette use.

These actually worsens the effect of both diabetes and hypertension, not necessarily causing but definitely predisposes to worsening of the effects of diabetes and high blood pressure on the body in general including the kidneys. Alcohol intake is implicated especially in liver disease which can lead to kidney disease. Various recreational drugs are also implicated which also leads to various diseases that can ultimately affect the kidneys. Another very important habit in our society today is insufficient amount of water intake with excessive amount of sugar intake. These have opposing effects, while water being a hydrating substance and sugar drinks being dehydrating substances. These have a very strong implication for kidney especially acute kidney disease.

How Common is Kidney Disease?

Kidney disease can either be acute or chronic. Chronic kidney disease is prevalent in one to two of every nine individuals between the age of 18 to 75 in the United States and as noted above, most common cause is diabetes and hypertension. Acute kidney disease is not as common as chronic kidney disease but its incidence is very high as opposed to prevalence since it is usually reversible. Most common form, especially in the out-patient happens as a result of the dehydration. However, in in-patient, it is more common as the results of sepsis, surgical procedures and of course these depend more on the specific hospital setting in question.

Redundancy of Kidneys

We were given by Almighty God two kidneys. I guess God saw it fit for us to have spare parts because we can successfully live with one kidney and actually donate one kidney to those who need kidneys. In fact, we can function with as little as one-quarter to one-eighth of a kidney.

Screening for kidney disease occurs in any good primary care physician office and when you consider the fact that kidney replacement therapy typically occurs when the kidney function is less than 15% and most cases less than 10% and many cases less than 5%. We find lots of redundancy in kidney function of 100%. What I mean by this is, if it takes a kidney function of 100% to go down to 10% before the need for kidney replacement therapy is the case, then that very large area of no disease or minimal symptoms and sign of disease becomes very apparent. This can either be seen as a good thing or not so good thing. A good thing in the fact that there are no symptoms and signs for quite a while. But it is a bad thing because there are no symptoms for a quite a while, which results in no action being taken on the part of the patient because he is not incentivized to do so. If on the other hand there was kidney pain as you get chest pain when you have heart disease, then there will be more incentive to do something to prevent worsening the kidney function.

Resilience of the Kidneys

The kidneys have synthetic and excretory functions. With kidney function at 10%, a patient can still function at this level for a while, sometimes a few years, which shows the resilience of the kidneys. Like the kidney's excretory ability (i.e. it's ability to get rid of waste), despite requiring oral replacement therapy, the kidney synthesizing ability (i.e. it's ability to make things) will work at normal levels once the function is regained. Most organs that have an acute insult resulting in scar formation tend to worsen slowly over time but with kidney function, this is actually not the case as there are really no symptoms till about 70 -75% function is lost.

More recently it has been found that exponentially over time, as in other organs, the resultant scars from acute insults do result in chronic deterioration of the kidneys but again this happens very, very slowly over time.

That is the end of chapter one. In the next chapter we will be discussing how you know you have kidney disease and what you can do about it.

CHAPTER TWO

How do you know you have kidney disease and what can you do about it

Symptoms of Kidney Disease

Symptoms of kidney disease are unfortunately not experienced until the disease is advanced especially in the chronic cases, i.e. chronic kidney disease. In acute kidney injury, sometimes because of the acuity of the kidney injury there are certain symptoms such as:

- Fatigue
- Difficulty in breathing
- Malaise
- Generalized body swelling
- Uncontrolled blood pressure.

You also have some symptoms of the disease that actually cause the kidney failure to develop. The disease may be disease such as urosepsis - that is kidney infection, in which case you have symptoms of burning on urination, urgency of urination, lower abdominal pain, back pain. These are all symptoms of the disease that caused the acute kidney injury. But with the chronic kidney disease, there are usually no symptoms. It is always interesting how patients that are referred to me for worsening kidney function always complain that they have no idea why they were referred because they have no symptoms. This is always the point that I educate them about as this has very large implications in patients compliance with therapy and follow up. As noted above when there's no incentive to follow up on your disease because there are no symptoms, the tendency is not to follow up.

Signs of Kidney Disease

As noted above with symptoms, signs are also more evident in advanced kidney disease especially when the disease is chronic. Signs we find depend on the cause of kidney disease, certain signs are noted with kidney failure although these signs could be found in many other diseases. Like:

- generalized body swelling
- crackles in the lungs on examination
- pallor of the mucous membranes
- uncontrolled blood pressure

 Other signs could be found depending on the etiology and the actual kind of kidney disease that exists such as:
- rashes found in interstitial nephritis (an inflammatory kidney disease)
- abdominal fullness found in polycystic kidney disease (an inherited condition that results in multiple cysts in both kidneys sometimes resulting in failure of the kidneys).

In acute kidney injury, certain ominous signs signify the need for a kidney replacement therapy such as:
- pericardial rub, which is a sound heard over the heart signifying inflammation of the lining of the heart
- asterixis where there is flapping of outstretched hands, usually signifying the existence of high levels of uremic toxins although you can also find this sign evident in the case of liver disease, as well.

-

Diagnosis of Kidney Disease

Various modalities are employed, most common is by a blood test measuring creatinine levels. This is actually a muscle protein, which is found in the blood in certain quantities and is cleared by the kidneys in a predictable fashion such that its level in the blood is reflective of actual kidney function. Other modalities could be by urine where the clearance is calculated based on a 24-hour urine collection. This is not quite the case anymore because of a formula that exists and allows us to calculate the 24-hour on the creatinine clearance by measuring the serum creatinine.

Radiological studies can be done to evaluate and help diagnose kidney disease, specifically the kidney ultrasound which further illuminates the total picture. Kidney biopsy is occasionally needed for definitive diagnosis of kidney disease. Rarely a CT scan can be used to diagnose kidney disease as well and other modalities are used to investigate the cause of kidney disease such as blood cultures, chest x-rays and more specific tests we use to further illuminate the course of kidney failure, specifically inflammatory causes of kidney failure.

Management of Kidney Disease

Management depends on whether this is acute or chronic kidney disease. For acute management, it actually consists of reversing the causative factors, as well as volume expansion to increase kidney perfusion, which is a very strong determinant of kidney function. Occasionally, immuno-suppression will be needed if the etiology of the kidney failure in question is thought to be due to an autoimmune response or hyper-immune response. Sometimes, just relieving the obstruction of the urine flow may result in reversal of kidney failure. Occasionally, there is a need for renal replacement therapy i.e. dialysis while the kidney recovers from the acute insult.

For chronic kidney disease, controlling the factors that cause the chronic kidney disease to occur become important such as lowering the blood pressure in patients that have hypertension and controlling blood sugar levels in patients that have diabetes. Lifestyle changes to effect reversal of blood sugar and blood pressure also become important and general improvement in kidney function has a lot of other lifestyle changes that occur independent of the effects on diabetes and blood pressure. Managing complications that arise from sub-optimal kidney function, also form part of the management of chronic kidney disease. These include management of problems with acid excretion into the urine, bone disease and anemia amongst others.

Prognosis of Kidney Disease

Prognosis is usually better for acute than chronic disease because acute is usually reversible while in chronic disease is usually not as forgiving. With chronic causes of disease that require renal replacement therapy, once this is started, there usually is little chance of renal recovery that exists. Unfortunately, this statement usually translates to, "I know once I start dialysis I will never get off of it, so I don't want to start." This gives the impression that dialysis itself results in an irreversible kidney failure but this is a clear case of which came first, the chicken or the egg. It is very important to realize that dialysis is an amazing procedure that exists and is utilized for various situations. One of them being irreversible kidney failure. Unfortunately because of this, it is seen as a cause of irreversible kidney failure as opposed to management of already established irreversible kidney failure. With acute causes of disease, renal replacement therapy is usually a bridge that is used to bridge the gap between kidney failure and kidney recovery.

What Can I Do About My Kidney Disease?

The most important thing to realize is that you can change your prognosis. Lifestyle changes can result in reversal of most common causes of chronic kidney disease and in all cases can definitely result in its retardation of progression. Increased hydration protects the kidney from the effects of many medications, treatments and procedures as well as surgery. Increased hydration with the consequent volume expansion is very protective of the kidney. Compliance with your nephrologist and clearing with him regarding any medications prescribed becomes very important.

Things Don't Just Happen, They Happen Just

This statement has sparked a little controversy whenever I say it. Whatever disease you are diagnosed with, your attitude towards everything will make you grow as a result of the situation you are in, or diminish as a result of the situation you're in. The likelihood of you beating any disease is much higher if you take the road of high responsibility and find out how you actually contributed to its happening and as a result of that process of finding out how you contributed to its happening, you also find out what you can do to reverse it or to prevent it from happening again. Sometimes you will not quite find out how you contributed to it or what role you had to play in acquiring the disease but your attitude of owning it and searching for your contribution to its occurrence will definitely lead you to finding out how you can either reverse it or prevent it from happening again or in many cases, prevent it from happening to your family members or those that you love. In effect, you grow as a result of the disease because of the attitude you have adopted.

This brings us to the end of chapter two. In the next chapter we will be discussing the patient who has been told they may need dialysis soon.

CHAPTER THREE

I have been told my kidneys are to the point that I may need dialysis soon. Now what do I do?

Worsening Kidney Function

When you are told you have worsening kidney function, make sure you are getting your doctor to discuss with you why this could be happening. Sometimes it is important to really get your doctor to commit to explain it to you, as not all doctors are naturally inclined to do so especially given the volume of patients that are seen every day by doctors but you can effectively accomplish this, again, with the right attitude where you create a scenario where your doctor actually WANTS to discuss with you as opposed to HAS to discuss with you. It is also important to become extreme about doing things to stop and reverse the progression of disease. These things are usually lifestyle changes that would help put you on a different trajectory than you're currently on, or than the trajectory that has landed you where you are currently as regards to your kidney disease. Many lifestyle changes which has been alluded to already and will continue being alluded to in this book will include decreasing fat intake as well as starch intake and increasing vegetables, fruits, and legumes, monitoring the phosphorus very closely with the legumes. Also decreasing sugary drink intake and increasing hydration with water, eliminating cigarette smoking and minimizing alcohol intake can also bring lifestyle changes. Physical activity on a regular basis, preferably daily or at least six days a week twice a day also becomes very important. Medications prescribed and over-the-counter medications are also very common culprits of progressive kidney function deterioration. So again, clearing with your nephrologist any medications prescribed to you is a very prudent habit to have. Also, when these changes are expected by you or your nephrologist, always ask your nephrologist to please repeat the labs to make sure a lab error has not occurred.

What Can You Do?

Most important thing for you to do is to educate yourself. Again, your attitude is paramount. Your responsibility level, the higher it is, the more results you get. So with this very high responsibility level, use your nephrologist as a resource. Note, I did not say give your nephrologist the responsibility of educating you. No. I said use your nephrologist as a resource. Take responsibility in getting your nephrologist to educate you. The nephrologist usually is a pretty bright person who is well-versed in his field and even if he doesn't know the answers to the questions you asked, he has a very large capacity on how to find out. Again, own your situation, and don't blame anyone else. With this level of responsibility, it's amazing what doors open up to you. By owning your situation, everyone - especially your doctors will do everything possible to help you through the situation. However, when you blame others, such as blaming the doctors for not treating you or for not finding out what the problem is, you decrease their resolve to help you. You reduce the chances of them actually being able to help you.

Getting Ready for Dialysis

Once you are consistently at a point where your GFR is less than 20 ml per minute, dialysis education should start. Important to be ready for kidney replacement therapy (dialysis) while you do everything you can to stay away from it i.e. getting ready for actual kidney replacement therapy while you're doing everything you need to be doing to prevent needing kidney replacement therapy. As we discussed above, everything with the lifestyle changes becomes very important to avoid your kidneys failing to the point where you need kidney replacement therapy, otherwise managing the complications that arise from the kidneys being at that stage of kidney disease.

There should be discussion then about the modality of dialysis to be employed. At this point, it is always very important to discuss modalities of treatment that are not frequently employed.

Unfortunately, when dialysis essentially creeps up on many patients and there is no education given before it is actually started, they almost invariably employ the modality of in-center hemodialysis. Home therapies are actually the preferred modality when education is employed because this helps keep the patients more functional day-to-day. In day-to-day living, activities of daily living where they are able to resume work have independence and autonomy of their care, so education about modality is really, really stressed there.

Preserving one's arm for vascular access, i.e. access to the blood that needs to be cleaned by dialysis, becomes very important. When blood is drawn for lab work or infusions are given for various reasons such as, intravenous iron, this results in damaging of veins that are very important, whose preservation is actually very important for the creation of the ideal access. This is referred to as the arteriovenous fistula, which consists of a vein being arterialized by an artery that has been connected to it surgically, such that the heart effectively pumps blood through the connecting artery into the vein that it is connected to. This portion of the vein is used to access the blood which would now be flowing at a faster rate than the typical venous blood would be flowing.

The advantage of this is that it serves to have the hybrid of the vein and the artery. If the artery was accessed for blood flow through the dialysis machine then the parts of the body being supplied by the artery will be still out of blood. Since there is no damming effect that pumped blood through the dialysis machine would clot very easily and various other complications may arise as they have in the past while this was being developed. Another very important step at this point is getting listed on the kidney transplant list. Once the GFR is less than 20, there should be a discussion about getting listed for a kidney transplant, and also discussions about testing of potential candidates for living related donor or unrelated donor.

Medications

Medications should be brought to every doctor visit. Patients are always surprised when I insist on this but the advantage of this becomes clear, if at every doctor visit, the doctor is asked to go through the medications and specifically asked if each one as it's brought up is still needed and the potential side effects of the medication is discussed. Compliance with medications becomes important as well and compliance is increased if the medication in question is understood and all the potential side effects clearly discussed. Medications are also very important for decreasing the morbidity that results from the GFR being less than 20, specifically acids in the blood, which results from decrease in acids dumping by the diseased kidney. Acids un-neutralized in the blood results in their need to be buffered by bone and by muscle and this leads to deterioration in the integrity, function, strength and overall health.

In order to neutralize certain toxins not being eliminated or add certain things not being synthesized in adequate quantities, pill burden may actually increase. Again, education becomes very important here in discussion with the nephrologist, such that compliance is maintained. When you know better, you tend to do better. When you do better, you tend to have more of what you want and less of what you don't want.

Education

When you have increased your responsibility level, education will be prioritized much higher. Again, I insist and emphasize, for you to use your nephrologist as a resource. Anything you learn from anywhere or anyone other than your nephrologist should be run by him or her. Use him as a filter of your information. Learn what you need to do, or stop doing, to have the best quality of life while on dialysis, while at the same time learning what to do to prevent needing dialysis. Again, it is a very different scenario than most diseases, because you have to think on two different levels. On one level, what you need to be doing, or not doing, to prevent your kidneys failing and needing dialysis. But on a different level, what you need to be doing to prevent having a poor quality of life on dialysis should you need it. Dialysis represents the only situation where a failed organ can be effectively replaced by a machine. No other organ failure exists in modalities like this, which is why unlike other organ failure, where you are just thinking in terms of preventing the organ from failing for self-preservation and to avoid death. In this case, you have to think to prevent the organ from failing, but also to have a good quality of life should the organs fail and you need the lifelong procedure in question, i.e. dialysis.

You and your Nephrologist

At this stage it is important to have a relationship with your nephrologist, a very good relationship with your nephrologist. If you don't trust him or you don't have faith in the care you are getting from him or her, get a second opinion. Don't feel the need to stay in an environment where you are not getting the care you feel you need or you have not developed any level of trust because of mistakes or a lack of discussion, communication. Every physician should be comfortable with you getting someone else's opinion in the care being given. If they are not, don't get a second opinion, get another nephrologist. Compliance with your nephrologist is key which is why your relationship with your nephrologist is very important, because your relationship with your nephrologist will either encourage or discourage compliance with the care being given and the suggestions being given for your care. As noted earlier, running everything, especially medications prescribed, by your nephrologist is very important. Use him as a resource.

Mindset

The right mindset helps you grow from your situation as opposed to the converse. A very interesting book written by Carol Dweck called Mindset talks about the difference between a fixed mindset and a growth mindset. A growth mindset is the mindset that results in you being able to essentially do everything to grow as a result of any situation as opposed to a fixed mindset, where you literally shrink in situations that are suboptimal, that are not comfortable. So with a growth mindset, people seize the chance to learn, knowing that stretching can make you do the impossible. They thrive when they stretch themselves and challenge and interest work hand-in-hand. People with a fixed mindset thrive when they have things safely within their grasp, losing interest when they are not feeling smart or talented when challenged. With a fixed mindset they feel smart when they are flawless right away, making no mistakes and things are easy. But with a growth mindset, they feel great when they learn something over time and confront and overcome challenges and do something they couldn't do before.

With a fixed mindset, they expect ability to show up without effort. The pressure of the fixed mindset doesn't allow people to become but only to already be. So every test of success defines them now and any future ability is thwarted as opposed to the growth mindset where their tests or success don't define them now. With the fixed mindset, they seek instant validation showing that they are superior or set apart from the rest or entitled. The word "failure" is referred to as a noun as opposed to a verb, such that someone's success becomes your failure and they are constantly looking to improve their self-esteem by looking for people or situations worse than theirs or blaming others for theirs. Their identity becomes their success or their failure.

The growth mindset allows people to enjoy what they are doing no matter how difficult and get to the top as a by-product of what they are doing not because they were striving to get there.

So the internal monologue with the growth mindset goes like this. How can I learn from this? How can I improve? So their aim is always to get better not to be seen or known as better. They don't focus on success and failure as much as the process.

Ultimately with a growth mindset, their heads are not filled with negative or self-limiting thoughts, or a fragile sense of belonging and they don't let people define them.

With the right mindset, you will come out better for the experience, not worse. You will also encourage people with a similar mindset to yours to gravitate to you and this makes for a much richer and fuller life.

This brings us to the end of chapter three. In the next chapter, we will be delving more into the world of dialysis with the patient just being started on dialysis.

CHAPTER FOUR

I was just started on dialysis. Now what?

Starting dialysis

Depending on the modality chosen, dialysis initiation may have to be in the hospital or preferably within a comprehensive out-patient system where you have a dialysis unit next to the doctor's office and next to the access center. Education about what to expect should have already happened as noted earlier. Always ask questions, questions, questions, questions. Everything should be explained to you, anything you don't understand, ask. Usually dialysis is started when uremic symptoms or signs are apparent such as nausea, vomiting, fluid overload with lots of generalized swelling and difficulty breathing. These are symptoms and signs that reflect the buildup of toxins in your blood to dangerously high levels. We prefer that these symptoms and signs are in their early stages and not florid, in which case they will be deemed unstable and then would have to be hospitalized and stabilized.

Prior to this, the patient should have been seen on a monthly or sometimes one or two weekly basis. Sometimes dialysis is started because the lab work dictates it, it is usually when the BUN is over 100, especially if this has happened acutely, going from 70 to 130 for instance. A typical first dialysis treatment is usually shorter and slower, then this progressively increases on a daily basis for a total of three treatments. This is done this way in order to help the patient transition with minimal symptoms. Sudden symptoms may arise if more fluids than is appropriate is removed very early in the dialysis journey, or if the clearance occurs too quickly with high blood flow rates. Patient may experience cramping or extreme light-headedness, but these symptoms are minimized and essentially prevented when started as noted above.

How can I avoid the dialysis drain?

The kidney removes fluid and clears toxins through the day, everyday for 24 hours of the day. Depending on modality of dialysis, the shifts of fluids and toxins tends to be less gradual and more aggressive, especially if the modality of in-center hemodialysis three days a week is chosen. The best way to avoid the dialysis drain then is to decrease the amount of fluid gained between the treatments. That way less fluid has to be removed during dialysis, essentially or effectively reducing the fluctuations in the fluid amount in the body. You can liken this to driving a car. When you're driving you are essentially moving the steering wheel, very slightly to the left and very slightly to the right many times a minute. Very rarely do you move extremely to the left or extremely to the right. This is usually done to avoid something at the last minute, like something crossing the road all over sudden and it results in very sharp swerves or accidents. Very rarely is it done in a normal movement of a car from one destination to another. So that smooth, slight fluctuation to the left and to the right of the steering wheel guides the car from point A to point B with very few swerves on the road.

The same could be said for dialysis, if you are able to remove a little bit of fluid because you only put on a little bit of fluid in between the treatments, you avoid the dialysis drain. But if you have to remove a lot of fluid during dialysis because you put a lot of fluid on in between the treatments then the dialysis drain and other complications ensue. Having said this, more time on dialysis results in less drain no matter how much fluid is put on. The longer you spend on dialysis, the slower the rate of fluid removal and it is actually the rate of fluid removal as opposed to the amount of fluid removed that results in the symptoms of the dialysis drain.

Education

Different pairs of shoes are being worn when you start dialysis, you just have to learn how to walk in them. In other words, you can resume your life normally once you start dialysis but as with a new pair of shoes, you have to learn to walk in these new shoes comfortably again and this is where education becomes paramount. You should ask questions from your tech, dialysis tech, from your RN as to why they are doing what they are doing. As to what they want to give you through your IV line. Everything should be explained to you. Ask questions. Have a high responsibility level such that you don't feel they need to tell you but you feel you need to ask them to please tell you. Your social support system should also be educated, so encourage your social support system, that is your family members to ask questions from the RN, from the tech, from the nephrologist. You should know your numbers and what they mean. You should know your numbers, referring to your lab results especially your hemoglobin, your potassium, phosphorous, iron levels, urea clearance, calcium, bicarb, dry weight, blood flow, albumin, blood pressure. These are all numbers you should constantly be asking for. The report card is typically given in most units and this should be discussed with your nephrologist and the rest of your dialysis team.

The ideal dialysis unit

The ideal dialysis unit is one where you feel comfortable. The staff has to be in total communication with you, explaining to you what they're doing, why they're doing what they're doing, what they're giving you and your numbers. The environment has to be very clean. Please don't hesitate to point out on cleanliness in your environment of dialysis as this is very important for your health and effective, efficient and successful dialysis. Ideally your nephrologist should be close by being able to see you during your treatments as frequently as possible but definitely being accessible to your nurses and techs throughout your treatment.

An access center should also be accessible such that you are able to be kept out of the hospital and any issues with your access, i.e. your arteriorvenous fistula, your arteriorvenous graft or your permcath, all accesses to your blood that needs to be dialysed as well as your peritoneal catheter, if you are on PD, should all be able to be fixed and managed in an access center in the outpatient setting. The plan is to keep you out of the hospital.

Also look for a unit to add value to you. This is more likely to happen as noted above if you have a high responsibility level such that you actually encourage people to add value to you. The tendency to have value added to you is much higher if you add value to others. This happens with the right attitude and of course, as earlier noted, a growth mindset.

You and your Nephrologist

As noted earlier, make sure you develop a relationship with your nephrologist. If you don't trust him or you don't have faith in the care that is being provided to you, get another opinion. Let him know you are getting another opinion and if he or she has a problem with that, get another nephrologist. Compliance with his guidance is very important, so again, you must have the right nephrologist whom you have a relationship with. Anything you are uncomfortable about, in the unit you are in, should be discussed with your nephrologist. Any medication changes should also be discussed. Any procedures to be undertaken by other physicians, other specialists, should also be discussed with your nephrologist. Again, use him as your main resource.

The dialysis team

The ideal dialysis team consists of the nephrologist, nurses which may include director of nursing, floor RNs, the dialysis techs, dietitian and a social worker. Occasionally, depending on the unit, there may also be a clinical educator and a lifestyle coach. With this team, education should be high priority. Use them as resources in addition to your nephrologist but whatever you learn from anybody else other than your nephrologist, run by your nephrologist. The ideal dialysis team should work in total cohesion effectively to provide an awesome dialysis experience for you.

Dialysis till…

Dialysis replaces kidney function until you get another kidney or your kidney recovers. Unfortunately, most people will pass away before they get a kidney transplant. One out of every four patients on dialysis would have passed away before the end of the year. Decrease the risk of being that one of those four patients by being compliant and educated. This is more likely to be the case if you have owned your situation and have developed a very high responsibility level with a growth mindset.

This brings us to the end of chapter four. In the next chapter, we will be discussing hospitalization of the patient on dialysis.

CHAPTER FIVE

Hospitalization and the patient on dialysis

Commonest reason for hospitalization of the patient on dialysis

Commonest reasons of hospitalization of the patient on dialysis are related to dialysis itself. Most commonly patients are hospitalized for volume overload, where they go into congestive heart failure because of fluid that has built up in their lungs and giving them a hard time to breath. This usually happens as a result of salt intake, some non-compliance with dietary restrictions, especially salt and fluid intake or missing dialysis treatments or insufficient dialysis treatment. Next common reason is access dysfunction in the form of a clotted access, an access just not working properly or an infected access, usually a catheter either for hemodialysis or for peritoneal dialysis. Also infection of the actual peritoneum is another common reason for the patients on peritoneal dialysis to be admitted. Another common reason for admission, although not as common as those noted above, are syncopal episodes, the patient actually passing out while on dialysis. This usually happens as a result of fluid removal being excessive because excessive fluid was gained and the patient was not able to tolerate the removal of the fluid he gained. Occasionally, these would happen from a cardiac episode or a cardiac event. Another reason why patients on dialysis are admitted is uncontrolled high blood pressure.

How can you avoid being hospitalized as a patient receiving dialysis?

As referred to earlier, being hospitalized can be avoided. This is more likely to happen if you are able to:

- locate a dialysis facility that is able to get you extra hemodialysis treatments if you need it quite quickly.
- To get you to an access center to have your access fixed if there is a problem with it.
- have prompt communication between yourself and your PD or hemodialysis nurse.

There is wisdom in having a facility closer to your nephrologist's clinic.

Common causes of hospitalizations of patients on dialysis not related to dialysis

There are many reasons why patients on dialysis may end up in the hospital other than reasons related to dialysis. Part of this results from the depressed immune function of patients that are on dialysis which is why everyone should have the flu vaccine and pneumonia vaccine. Common reasons for hospitalization of these patients includes:

- Chest pain which is usually taken more seriously because kidney disease is a strong risk factor for coronary artery disease.
- Infections such as pneumonia or even sepsis.
- Diabetes complications, either high sugars or low sugars.

These are the more common reasons why patients on dialysis are admitted to the hospital not relating to dialysis.

Effects of being on dialysis on your hospital experience

When hospitalized as a patient receiving dialysis, your experience is affected by the amount of dialysis experience of the hospital staff. Education of the hospital nurses is very important. Timing of procedures with inpatient hemodialysis is also very important. They should be coordinated by dialysis nurses as well as the floor nurses. The dietitian should always be consulted to add to the knowledge base of the dialysis patient as well as the nurses caring for the patient. Medication should always be adjusted for being on dialysis, so the nephrologist should always be consulted. Ask questions before accepting any offered treatment and run everything by your nephrologist.

Dialysis in the hospital

Own it! Dialysis while in the hospital can be very smooth but for this to happen you have to actually own it. Ask questions, always ask questions. Make sure you understand everything that is being done to you and everything that is been given to you. Know your numbers, when you know your numbers in the out-patients, you can relay this to the in-patient nurse, who should have access to this information but is more likely to use that information if it comes from you, in addition to obtaining it from your unit. Ask for extra treatments in the hospital, if you need it. Know your dialysis medications i.e. whatever they give you on dialysis and the doses. Know what PD bags you use and your prescription.

Ensure smooth transition from hospital dialysis to outpatient dialysis

Again, education is key and the best way to get educated is by asking questions. Didn't I already say this? Know when your next treatment is supposed to be. Discuss with the social worker in the hospital regarding transportation and timing of treatments. Discuss with your social support system which days are most convenient for everyone for you to receive dialysis and involve them in all your decision making. If you don't have a permanent access for hemodialysis i.e. arteriovenous fistula or graft, have a plan to have one done in the very near future before you leave the hospital. Before dialysis, go and visit your unit and meet the staff before actually having to go there for dialysis.

You and your Nephrologist

Again, as discussed earlier, discuss with your nephrologist the game plan to avoid your admission to the hospital. Make this a very strong focus, your quality of life improves with a lower incidence of being re-admitted to the hospital. Whenever you are admitted to the hospital always find out what could have been done to prevent this admission. Find out what you need to do to prevent the admission and let your nephrologist know you feel you own the situation, but you want his help to prevent it from happening again. Remember, don't look to blame, but own the situation so that you have the power to prevent it from happening again as opposed to blaming, in which case you have given away the power to prevent things from happening to you.

This brings us to the end of chapter five. For the next chapter, will be delving into what happens beyond yourself on dialysis.

CHAPTER SIX

Beyond yourself on dialysis (the awesome dialysis patient)

Encourage an awesome support system

This again is related to your attitude and growth mindset by having a high responsibility level and owning a situation, you are more likely to encourage your family members to form a strong support group around you. You are also more likely to inspire your friends and family to form the strongest support system for you. Again, it is all about your attitude and mindset. Do not feel entitled to have a social support system, on the other hand, feel privileged and blessed to have one and appreciate them.

Encourage your relatives to be screened

As a patient on dialysis, your family members are predisposed to having kidney disease. Having them screened for this regularly, at least yearly is a very prudent course to take. Encourage them to have lifestyle changes that will prevent diseases, especially chronic diseases from manifesting themselves, and remind them that kidney disease has no signs or symptoms until the disease is advanced. Screening is very simple and is done at most doctor visits in the form of blood tests and urine tests.

Accept the amazing gift of a kidney from your family member

The kidney transplant is the preferred way to manage end-stage kidney disease. Mortality rate is much higher than patients on with dialysis, quality of life is also much better than patients on dialysis. Accept the gift of a kidney even from your children. Your trust of your nephrologist becomes very important as he assembles a kidney transplant team for you, they will be in charge of screening your loved ones to determine whether or not they can actually afford to give a kidney away to you. Trust the system, if your loved one cannot afford to have his kidney donated to you the kidney transplant team will tell you this. It is always erroneous when a kidney transplant is not done because the patient feels a family member should not have to "suffer losing their kidney to him". Trust the system, if they can afford to give you a kidney, take it. You will be, as well as the donor, better for it so trust the system. Your mortality rate and your quality of life increases as a result of a kidney transplant. And you need to see it as being given a new lease on life. Again, both you and the donor would be better off for it.

Make your dialysis team want to take care of you

The best leadership style is one in which you make people want to do things as opposed to having to do things. In dialysis you are more likely to function as an ideal leader of your care if you own your situation, with a high responsibility level and a growth mindset encouraging people to want to do things for you as opposed to them feeling they have to do it for you. The sense of entitlement and the behavior that goes a long with it is very discouraging and repulsive to people that are supposed to be taking care of you. The power of one refers to your attitude towards any relationship where you give 100% of yourself, expecting 0% in return. This way you always win because it depends totally on you and on no one else, again it is all about your attitude and mindset.

Become an educator

As your responsibility level rises so does your growth mindset and the tendency is you will educate yourself even more. Educate yourself with the intention of educating others i.e. your family, other patients, even your caretakers. When you educate yourself with intention to teach others, you tend to educate yourself even more effectively and efficiently and when you know more you become more. When you become more, you do more and when you do more, you have more of what you want and less of what you don't want. Most people unfortunately in your position do not do this. They do not educate themselves but they are more likely to be educated if they are educated by you because they can relate to you better than they can relate to anyone else not receiving dialysis, even their own nephrologist.

Engage research

Engage your nephrologist to enroll you in studies. Patients on dialysis form a very unique population that require more study to improve and create anything that will increase your quality of life. The fact that you already come to a clinical setting three times a week or you are in a setting at home on a regular basis, that affords for clinical study makes it very convenient for you to participate in studies already. There is also compensation which also exists for the patient being studied. The likelihood of breakthrough technology and therapy is higher with a higher number of people willing to be studied.

Whatever you focus on, becomes bigger

Your responsibility level increases with the growth mindset, and owning your situation becomes more of a reality. The tendency then becomes to focus on the things you can impact, and focus much less on the things you cannot impact. What does this lead to? This leads to you being able to impact many more things, and the things you are not able to impact become less of an issue and less of a time waster. Whatever you focus on becomes bigger and more attainable, and definitely more fixable.

This brings us to the end of chapter six. We will be delving into the future of dialysis in the next chapter.

CHAPTER SEVEN

Future of dialysis

Dialysis journey

Dialysis has come a long way since the first dialyser in 1943. In the 1960s, bioethics committee were formed to decided who would receive hemodialysis and who would not. 50 years later there is essentially nobody that is refused dialysis and people are returning to work faster and living productive lives. Home therapy is encouraged for good reason as I alluded to earlier and people are learning to walk in their new shoes much quicker, much more effectively, so when you look at journey from 1943 till date, we have come a long way and the future is still bright.

Cost of dialysis

Dialysis remains a very important treatment to the healthcare system. Although it caters to less than 1% of CMS subscribers, it actually accounts for about 8% of the CMS dollars. The cost is increased mostly by the rate of hospitalization and this unfortunately is increased because of the perception that patients must be dialysed in the hospital, if they are in the ER for any problem, including problems for which the hospitalization is actually not necessary. Decreasing this hospitalization will bring about the biggest difference to the amount of money being spent on dialysis. Another factor that increases hospitalizations is the dialysis catheter. So increasing education and the patients being seen by the nephrologist early enough to impact them such that they don't need a catheter before starting dialysis will have very positive consequences on this burgeoning problem.

Dialysis here relative to other places

Dialysis in other countries such as Amsterdam and China have recorded better outcomes with decreased mortality rates than in the US. Various reasons have been touted for this. One of them being more contact with the nephrologist, in some cases the nephrologist is present at every treatment. Another factor that may have led to this is the percentage of patients that have diabetes as the cause for their ESRD, which is higher here in the States because of our diet than in other countries. However, another factor that has led to these findings would actually be the fact that we are more liberal, that is the United States, in our acceptance policy for placing patients on dialysis. Hence we have sicker patients or patients with higher comorbid conditions than in other countries. Conclusion here is that we provide excellent care in the United States but are more liberal with acceptance policy and the possibility of the nephrologist being at more treatments would result in a decrease in mortality rates in the United States.

Dialysis research

This is an area in which there is lots of research occurring. In the last few years, research has been increasing in various areas, specifically in health economics, early clinic research, late stage clinical trials, outcomes research, medical communication and bio-repository services. The research focuses on various aspects of the dialysis experience including various medications needed for specific situations, peculiar to patients on dialysis. Research is the way forward for dialysis and increases the chances of breakthrough therapy, resulting in improvement and quality of life, and much improvement in mortality of our patients on dialysis.

Dialysis accessibility

Dialysis accessibility only relates to in-center hemodialysis, as home therapies don't have this as an issue. Essentially with home therapies, you go to the units not more than twice a month. Low-access is defined based on driving time and this varies from country to country. But it has been found quality of life decreases and mortality increases if patients travel more than 60 minutes one way to the dialysis unit and tends to significantly increase if it is more than 30 minutes. The gradient of increase is even higher if it is more than 60 minutes one way. Solution to this is more home therapies for patients in areas with less accessibility and possibly the need for more comprehensive care, with dialysis units being close to the nephrology clinics.

Living with dialysis compared to 20 Years from now

In the past five to ten years, there has been renewed interest with advances in the sciences of nanotechnology and micro-fluids. This has resulted from various parts of this. Stem cells as a potential source of tissues and organs, has become an area of keen interest. WAK (wearable artificial kidneys) for hemodialysis or PD, is also a field for intense research and very hopeful advance has been made in this area. Nanotechnology applications, appliances, with the human nephron filter is also an area of keen research. Renal assist device with bio-artificial kidney has also been a large part of the news of this area. So looking at dialysis 20 years from now, we are hoping it will be different and much more convenient with improved quality of life and improved mortality rates for patients on dialysis.

Improvement in prognosis of the dialysis patient

Improvement in the outcome of a patient on dialysis is still needed, mortality rates are still unacceptable. Despite advances of the last 50 years, one out of very four patients is still unacceptable. Research is still strongly being carried out, lots of dollars being spent on creating better modalities of treatment. However, it's very important that it's realized by you the dialysis patient that your chance of survival and the improved quality of life is increased if you own it and have an increased level of responsibility and approach the care you're given with the power of one as noted above, with the growth mindset.

We have been able to cover the kidneys and the importance in disease, after which we delve into how you know you have kidney disease and what you can do about it. This was followed by knowing what to do when you have been told you are at the point you may need dialysis and then we discussed what you do after you have been started on dialysis. We were able to discuss hospitalization and the patient on dialysis and then we were able to eliminate going beyond yourself on dialysis. And finally, we talked about the future of dialysis.

Take action to achieve being in a nice, comfortable, and warm dialysis unit where there's awesome communication between yourself and your dialysis care providers, especially your nephrologist, and receiving such comprehensive care that hospitalization is very rarely required. The first step is call my office at 407-988-1065 and ask to speak to Shannon or Mimi and tell her, "I want to take advantage of Dr. Awosika's dialysis services," and she will get you all started and set up.

www.ingramcontent.com/pod-product-compliance
Lightning Source LLC
LaVergne TN
LVHW020100190726
843498LV00012B/1908